For Cat Lovers Everywhere:

Blessed are those who love cats,
for they shall never be lonely.

The Proverbial Cat

Published by Sellers Publishing, Inc.
161 John Roberts Road, South Portland, ME 04106
Visit us at www.sellerspublishing.com • E-mail: rsp@rsvp.com

© 2017 Sellers Publishing, Inc.
Artwork © 2017 Sydney Hauser

Text credits appear on page 64.

Printed and bound in China.

10 9 8 7 6 5 4 3 2 1

The Proverbial Cat

Animals are such agreeable friends, they ask no questions, they pass no criticisms.
~ George Eliot

Feline Inspirations by Sydney Hauser

SELLERS
PUBLISHING

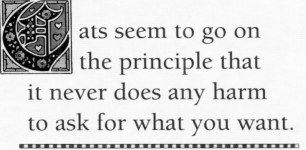ats seem to go on
the principle that
it never does any harm
to ask for what you want.

I put down my book, *The Meaning of Zen*, and see the cat smiling into her fur as she delicately combs it with her rough pink tongue. Cat, I would lend you this book to study but it appears you have already read it. She looks up and gives me her full gaze. Don't be ridiculous, she purrs, I wrote it.

Joy is in little things...
a little cat, a little book,
time spent reading in a cozy nook.

Louder he purrs, and louder,
in one glad hymn of praise
for all the night's adventures,
for quiet, restful days.
Life will go on forever,
with all that cat can wish:
warmth and the glad procession
of fish and milk and fish.

Who among us hasn't envied a cat's ability to ignore the cares of daily life and to relax completely?

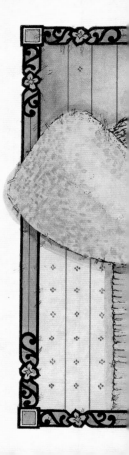

I would enjoy
the day more
if it started later.

No matter how much cats fight, there always seems to be plenty of kittens.

Abraham Lincoln

Who could believe
such pleasure from
a wee ball o' fur?

Since each of us
is blessed with only
one life, why not
live it with a cat?

God made the Cat
so that we might know
the pleasure of embracing the Lion.

I saw the most beautiful cat today. It was sitting by the side of the road, its two front feet neatly and graciously together. Then it gravely swished around its tail to completely and snugly encircle itself. It was so fit and beautifully neat, that gesture, and so self-satisfied — so complacent.

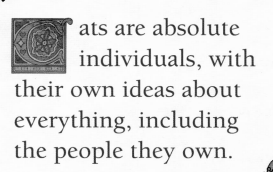ats are absolute individuals, with their own ideas about everything, including the people they own.

Feelings are everywhere, be gentle.

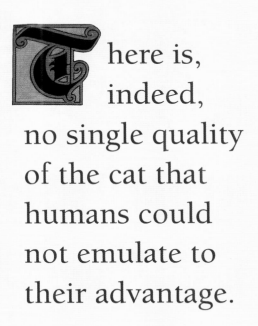

There is, indeed, no single quality of the cat that humans could not emulate to their advantage.

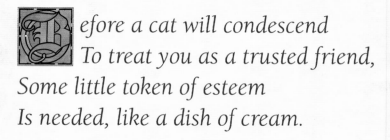

efore a cat will condescend
    To treat you as a trusted friend,
Some little token of esteem
Is needed, like a dish of cream.

A home·without·a·cat·
is·like·a·garden·
without·flowers·

Happy is
the home with at
least one cat.

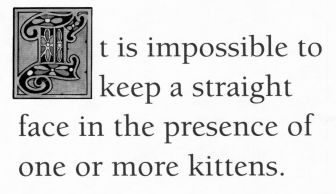It is impossible to keep a straight face in the presence of one or more kittens.

The smallest of
felines is a
·masterpiece·

Leonardo da Vinci

The phrase "domestic cat" is an oxymoron.

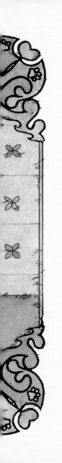

I'm only a cat,
and I stay in my place . . .
Up there on your chair,
on your bed, on your face!
I'm only a cat,
and I don't finick much . . .
I'm happy with cream
and anchovies and such!
I'm only a cat,
and we'll get along fine . . .
As long as you know
I'm not yours . . .
you're all mine!

A cat can purr
its way out
of *anything*.

To·err·is·human;
to·purr·is·feline.

Blessed are
those who love
cats, for they shall
never be lonely.

Cats are a
mysterious
kind of folk.
There is more
passing in their
minds than we
are aware of.

A cat is a **puzzle** for which there is no solution.

Wisdom comes to those who live with both feet (or all paws) on the ground.

Of all animals,
the cat alone
attains to the
contemplative life.

If cats could talk, they wouldn't.

A meow
massages
the heart.

There has never been a cat
Who couldn't calm me down
By walking slowly
Past my chair.

The ideal of calm of calm exists in a sitting cat.

Jules Renard

It's the simple things that make life so rich.

It is in a cat's
eyes that the
magic resides.

Cats are kindly masters,
just so long as you
remember your place!

Cats don't like change
without their consent.

A home without a cat,
a well-fed, well-petted,
and properly revered cat
may be a perfect home,
perhaps, but how can it
prove its title?

The cat goes out
And the cat comes back
And no one can follow
Upon her track.
She knows where she's going
She knows where she's been,
All we can do
Is to let her in.

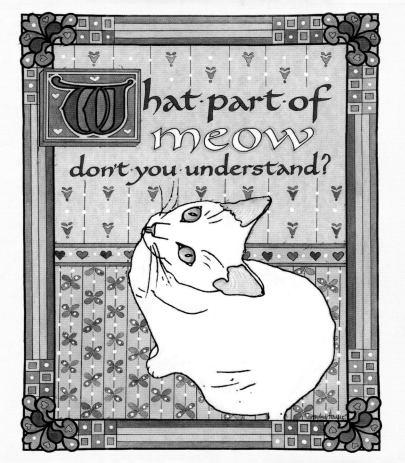

A cat's hearing apparatus
is built to allow the
human voice to
go easily in one ear
and out the other.

believe cats to be spirits come to Earth. A cat, I am sure, could walk on a cloud without coming through.

If you love something, set it free...
if it doesn't come back,
it was never meant to be.
if it does return, love it forever.

A big dust ball is the kitten

The cat was created
when the lion
sneezed.

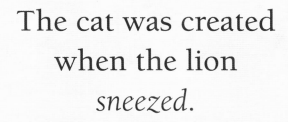

Way down deep,
we're all motivated
by the same urges.
Cats have the courage
to live by them.

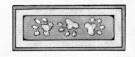

The heart which gives freely is never lonely.

*hen you're
special to a cat,
you're special indeed . . .
she brings to you
the gift of her preference
of you, the sight of you,
the sound of your voice,
the touch of your hand.*

*In a cat's
eyes,
all things
belong
to cats.*

The cat and it's housekeeping staff

reside here.

Credits:

p. 5 © Joseph Wood Krutch; p. 6 © Dilys Laing; p. 9 © Alexander Gray; p. 10 © Karen Fleisher; p. 13 Irish saying; p. 14 © Robert Stearns; p. 17 © Mary Morrow Lindburgh; p. 18 © John Dingman; p. 21 © Carl Van Vechten; p. 22 © T. S. Eliot; p. 25 Italian proverb; p. 26 © Cynthia E. Varnado; p. 29 author unknown; p. 30 © Donna McCrohan; p. 33 author unknown; p. 34 © Sir Walter Scott; p. 37 © Lizzie Stewart; p. 38 © Andrew Lang; p. 41 ©Stuart McMillan; p. 42 © Rod McKuen; p. 45 © Arthur Symons; p. 46 © Paul Gray; p. 49 © Samuel Clemens; p. 50 © Marchette Chute; p. 53 © Stephen Baker; p. 54 © Jules Verne; p. 57 Arabian proverb; p. 58 © Jim Davis; p. 61 © Leonore Fleisher; p. 62 English proverb.